Word Bird™ Bird

Makes Words
With Dog

The
**Child's
World**

Published in the United States of America by The Child's World®, Inc.
PO Box 326
Chanhassen, MN 55317-0326
800-599-READ
www.childsworld.com

Project Manager Mary Berendes
Editor Katherine Stevenson, Ph.D.
Designer Ian Butterworth

Library of Congress Cataloging-in-Publication Data
Moncure, Jane Belk.
Word Bird makes words with Dog : a short "o" adventure / by Jane Belk Moncure.
p. cm.
Summary: Word Bird and his friend Dog make up a variety of words,
and each new word leads them into a new activity.
ISBN 1-56766-900-X (lib. bdg.)
[1. Vocabulary. 2. Birds—Fiction. 3. Dogs—Fiction.] I. Title.
PZ7.M739 Wnd 2001
[E]—dc21
00-010895

Word Bird™ Bird™

Makes Words With Dog

by Jane Belk Moncure

illustrated by Chris McEwan

One morning, Word Bird
said, "I can make word
puzzles all by myself."

Word Bird put

d with og.

What did Word Bird make?

d og

Just then, Dog came over
to play.

"Hi, Dog."

"I can make word puzzles, too," said Dog. Dog put

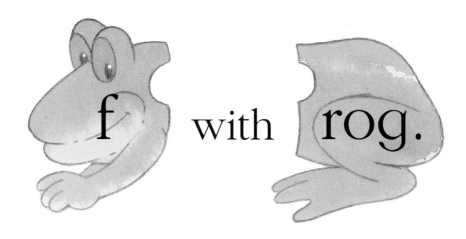

f with rog.

What word did Dog make?

frog

"Let's go to the pond and see the frogs," said Dog.

But there were no frogs
in the pond.

"Look," said Word Bird.
"There are polliwogs
in the pond. Someday
the polliwogs will
become frogs."

"What can we do now?"
asked Dog. Word Bird put

What did Word Bird make?

"Lets jog around the pond," said Dog. So they did.

Then they sat on a log.
"What can we do now?"
asked Dog.

Word Bird made another
word. Word Bird put

b   with   ox.

What did Word Bird make?

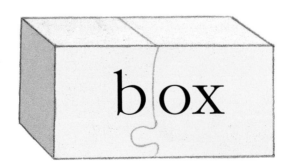

box

Then Dog made a word.
Dog put

f with ox.

What word did Dog make?

"Let's get a fox and put it in my box," said Dog.

But they could not find a fox.

They found

an ox

and an
ostrich.

And they found an otter, but still no fox.

"The foxes are hiding," said Dog.

Word Bird made another
word. Word Bird put

r with ocks.

"Guess the word,"
said Word Bird.

"Rocks," said Dog.

"Let's go back to the pond.
Maybe a fox is hiding
behind the rocks."

Dog looked behind
the rocks.

There was Fox!

Fox ran up and down
the rocks.

Dog could not catch Fox.
Dog could not put fox
in the box.

"What can we do now?"
asked Dog. Word Bird put

bl with ocks.

"What is the word?"
asked Word Bird.

"Blocks," said Dog.

"Let's build something with blocks," Word Bird said.

They built a doghouse out
of blocks.

Then they built a boat
dock out of blocks.

Suddenly, they heard
"Pop. Pop. Pop."

"What was that?"
asked Dog.

They hopped into the kitchen.

Mama was making something in a pot.

"Popcorn!" said Word Bird.
"Hot popcorn," said Dog.

After they ate all the
popcorn, they were
about to POP.

You can read more word puzzles with Word Bird.

l ock

h og

f og

cl ock

s ock

l ong

t op

s ong

st op

Now you can make some word puzzles.

```
           HPARX    +
                    E
                    MONCU


     MONCURE, JANE BELK
        WORD BIRD MAKES
     WORDS WITH DOG
                     Friends of the
                   Houston Public Library
```